Garfield sits around the house

BY: JIM DAVIS

BALLANTINE BOOKS · NEW YORK

Library of Congress Catalog Card Number: 83-90066
ISBN: 0-345-32011-5

Manufactured in the United States of America

First Edition: October 1983

23   24

A GARFIELD NIGHT...

MIDNIGHT SNACK

GARFIELD: © 1978 United Feature Syndicate, Inc.

BREAKFAST

HOW ARE YOU BOYS GOING TO GET OUT OF THE TREE?

I DON'T KNOW HOW I'M GETTING OUT OF THE TREE

© 1982 United Feature Syndicate, Inc. 1-20

AS FOR ODIE...

JIM DAVIS

HEY, GARFIELD, HOW ARE YOU GOING TO GET OUT OF THAT TREE?

1-21

JIM DAVIS

BOING!

BOING!

WHY, BY USING MY HEAD... AND JON'S, AND ODIE'S

© 1982 United Feature Syndicate, Inc.

KABOOM

I HATE
MONDAY

© 1982 United Feature Syndicate, Inc.

© 1982 United Feature Syndicate, Inc.

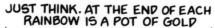

© 1982 United Feature Syndicate, Inc.

YOU KNOW, YOU'RE A VERY LUCKY CAT, GARFIELD

YOU HAVE JUST ABOUT EVERYTHING A CAT COULD WANT

YOU HAVE YOUR SANCTUM SANCTORUM

MY HIDEY-HOLE

YOU HAVE YOUR TEDDY BEAR

MY CONFIDANT

YOU HAVE YOUR DOG

MY SCRATCHING POST

JIM DAVIS   2-14

AND YOU HAVE ME, YOUR LOVING COMPANION

MY FOOD-FIXER AND LITTER BOX CHANGER

© 1982 United Feature Syndicate, Inc.

I DON'T BELIEVE I ATE THAT WHOLE BAG OF CAT FOOD

JIM DAVIS 2-17

I'D BETTER JOG SOME OF THIS TUMMY OFF

I REALLY DON'T LIKE MYSELF WHEN I'M THIS FAT

JIM DAVIS 2-18

SWIPE!

I CAN'T EVEN ENJOY THE SIMPLE PLEASURES IN LIFE

AHCHOO!
© 1982 United Feature Syndicate, Inc. 3-10

GESUNDHEIT
SNIFF

AND NOW, A WORD FROM OUR SPONSOR
3-11

ZOOM
© 1982 United Feature Syndicate, Inc.

WELCOME BACK

MMMPH FMOPH FWEEF

THAT IS CORRECT. IT IS TIME TO GET UP

MAD DOG! MAD DOG!

STAY OUT OF MY WHIPPED CREAM, ODIE

GARFIELD HAS THE UNIQUE ABILITY TO HEAR A CAN OPENER FROM ANYWHERE IN THE HOUSE

RRRRRRR

WHA...

© 1982 United Feature Syndicate, Inc.

3-21

JIM DAVIS

I LOVE SHOW BUSINESS. GIMME THE FULL MOON. GIMME THE FENCE

3-24

KAWHOCK!

© 1982 United Feature Syndicate, Inc.

GIMME THE BROKEN TEETH. GIMME THE MULTIPLE LACERATIONS

JIM DAVIS

'CAUSE MOMMA WAS A GREAT OLD GALLLL

♪MROOW♪

3-25

© 1982 United Feature Syndicate, Inc.

THANK YOU FOR THAT LARGE ROUND OF INDIFFERENCE

JIM DAVIS

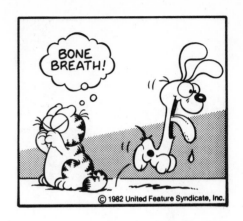

DON'T YOU DARE WALK ACROSS THE TABLE WITH THOSE MUDDY FEET

I MUST HAVE BLOWN A FUSE

© 1982 United Feature Syndicate, Inc.

JIM DAVIS

4-4

© 1982 United Feature Syndicate, Inc.

4-18

4.30

I GOTTA FIX THAT VERTICAL HOLD

WE'LL BE RIGHT BACK AFTER THIS WORD FROM OUR SPONSOR

5-1

SASQUATCH

WELCOME BACK

JiM DAViS 5-2

© 1982 United Feature Syndicate, Inc.

HURRY UP WITH THAT HAY, SON. SUPPER'S WAITIN'

5-7

JIM DAVIS

SON?

LONG TIME, NO FARM, HUH, JON?

WE HAD FUN VISITING THE FARM, DIDN'T WE, GARFIELD?

SPEAK FOR YOURSELF, JON

JIM DAVIS

5-8

IT'S GREAT GETTING BACK TO BASICS, PUTTING YOUR HANDS IN OLD MOTHER EARTH

BUT I'LL NEVER GET THESE FINGERNAILS CLEAN

A REAL MAN OF THE LAND

SPLAT

SPLOOSH

WHY IS IT CATS CHASE
BUTTERFLIES? IS IT
INSTINCT, OR IS IT
JUST STUPIDITY?

© 1982 United Feature Syndicate, Inc.

JIM DAVIS

PROBABLY
STUPIDITY

5-16

YAWN

© 1982 United Feature Syndicate, Inc.

WHAT HAPPENED TO YOU?

I GOT UP ON THE WRONG SIDE OF THE BED

JIM DAVIS 5-17

JIM DAVIS 5-18

CHUG!

YOU'RE A REAL BEAR UNTIL YOU'VE HAD YOUR FIRST CUP OF COFFEE, AREN'T YOU?

AND THEN I'M THE SWEETEST SO-AND-SO AROUND

© 1982 United Feature Syndicate, Inc.

(CLICK) **EEEEEEEE!**

(CLICK) YOU KNOW, PLEASURE MOTORS

(CLICK)

5-23

(CLICK) HI YUH, KIDS!

PICK A STATION AND STAY WITH IT, GARFIELD

CLICK!

JIM DAVIS

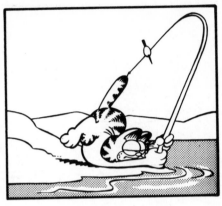

JIM DAVIS

6-2

© 1982 United Feature Syndicate, Inc.

JIM DAVIS

6-3

LAP
LAP
LAP

LAP
LAP

© 1982 United Feature Syndicate, Inc.

WAH-
CHOO!

WAH-
CHOO!

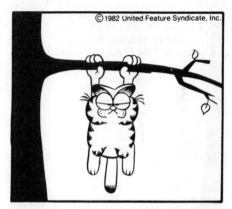

YAWN

YOU KNOW YOU'RE GETTING OLDER WHEN YOUR FAVORITE LATE NIGHT SHOW IS THE SIX O'CLOCK NEWS

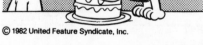

HELLO. I'M NERMAL, THE WORLD'S CUTEST KITTEN, HERE TO DO CUTE KITTEN THINGS IN ORDER TO CHARM THE PANTS OFF YOUR OWNER AND POINT OUT HOW UNCUTE YOU ARE

I HATE MONDAY

© 1982 United Feature Syndicate, Inc.

GIMME THAT

JIM DAVIS   6-22

I FAIL TO SEE WHAT'S SO CUTE ABOUT YARN

OR KITTENS, FOR THAT MATTER

© 1982 United Feature Syndicate, Inc.

JIM DAVIS   6-21

'SPLUT

DON'T YOU DARE LAUGH. I HATE IT WHEN SOMEONE HAS A LAUGH AT MY EXPENSE

JIM DAVIS

'SPLAT

IF I LAUGH, GARFIELD WILL KILL ME. IF I DON'T LAUGH, I'LL BURST

WAH HA HA HA!

© 1982 United Feature Syndicate, Inc.

6-27

HA HA HA, WHEEE

6-28

IT'S TIME YOU GO ON ANOTHER DIET, GARFIELD

JUST WHAT IS A DIET?

6-29

A DIET IS TOO LITTLE OF A GOOD THING. A DIET IS MAKING A MOLEHILL OUT OF A MOUNTAIN

A DIET IS THE SUBJECT OF A LOT OF STUPID PLATITUDES

© 1982 United Feature Syndicate, Inc.

THAT APPLE IS ALL YOU'RE GETTING FOR DINNER, GARFIELD

JIM DAVIS   7-2

© 1982 United Feature Syndicate, Inc.

GIMME FOOD. LOTS OF IT. AND RIGHT NOW

JIM DAVIS   7-3

YES, SIR

© 1982 United Feature Syndicate, Inc.

TWO ADJECTIVES NEVER USED TO DESCRIBE A CAT ARE: "WISHY" AND "WASHY"

7-4

IN OUR FAST-PACED WORLD, RELAXATION IS PRACTICALLY A LOST ART

7-5

JIM DAVIS

Z

PRACTICALLY

HERE YOU GO, GARFIELD

TABLE SCRAPS!

GARFIELD

JIM DAVIS

7-6

SPLAT!

THAT'S DOG FOOD

DON'T LOOK IN HERE, JON. IT'S NOT A PRETTY SIGHT

I WISH JON WOULD GET MARRIED

FWEEE

THE ONLY WAY HE KNOWS MY DINNER IS READY, IS WHEN IT SETS OFF THE SMOKE ALARM

© 1982 United Feature Syndicate, Inc.

© 1982 United Feature Syndicate, Inc.

JIM DAVIS

7-16

7-17

JIM DAVIS

I KNOW, I KNOW

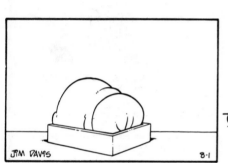

Here is the Paws, Incorporated staff—the faces behind the cat—with their noses to the grindstone, shoulders to the wheel, ears to the ground, and faces to the picture window.

Top row, left to right: Mike Fentz, Artist; Valette Hildebrand, Assistant Cartoonist; Larry Carmichael, Pilot; Ron Tuthill, Production Manager; Dave Kühn, Artist; Dave Davis, Artist; Brian Lum, Artist; and Kevin Campbell, Artist.

Bottom row, left to right: Dick Hamilton, Business Manager; Neil Altekruse, Artist; Linda Sissom, Office Manager; Jill Hahn, Licensing Assistant; Jim Davis, Garfield Creator; Sheila Bolduc, Traffic Manager; and Julie Hamilton, President.